THE LION BOOK OF
Two-Minute
PARABLES

Retold by
Elena Pasquali
Illustrated by
Nicola Smee

LION
CHILDREN'S

Contents

The Sower

When the crowds came to listen to Jesus, he often told them stories.

"Once," he said, "a man went out to sow seeds. Up and down the field he plodded, flinging handfuls of seeds.

"Some fell on the path. Birds swooped down and ate them.

"Some seeds fell on stony ground. The seeds soon sprouted, but the roots did not go deep.

"When the sun shone bright and hot, the seedlings drooped.

"Some seeds fell among thorn bushes. They soon grew, but the plants could not reach the light. They faded away.

"Other seeds fell on the good brown earth. They grew and produced a good harvest."

flop

peck peck

7

It was a good story, but even Jesus' best friends were puzzled. "What does it mean?" they asked.

"It's about the people who come and listen to me," said Jesus. "Some are like the seeds on the path. They hear my words but don't remember. It's as if the words were snatched away.

Gone

I give up

"Some are like the seeds on stony ground. They hear what I say. They try to obey. Then things get hard and they give up.

"Some are like the seeds among thorn bushes. They too try to obey my words. Then everyday worries get in the way.

Have to make money

Let's share

"Others are like the seeds on good brown earth. They hear my words. They obey them. Their lives are a harvest of good deeds."

The Merchant and the Pearl

"The most important thing in the world," said Jesus, "is being friends with God.

"What do you do if something is very important?

"Listen to this story.

pink pearls

black pearls

"There was once a merchant. He travelled
far and wide to find the best pearls.

white pearls

blue pearls

11

"One day, he had the chance to buy an amazing pearl.

"It was big.

"It was pure white.

"It was perfectly round.

"It was very expensive.

"The merchant knew it was the most valuable pearl in the world.

I have to afford it!

"He went off and sold all the pearls he had. Then he came back and bought the pearl that he really loved."

FOR SALE

Ooh!

Aah!

13

Building a Tower

Crowds of people came to listen to Jesus.

"Do you really want to follow me?" he asked. "Then you must love one another.

"You must forgive the wrong things that people do to you.

"You may find it hard."

The people began to wonder if this was a good idea.

Not sure

Hmm

"It's like with any big plan," said Jesus.
"Imagine someone who dreams of building a tower.

*It will be
the tallest!*

"First of all, he must count the cost.

"If he doesn't, he may run out of money. The tower will be half finished.

"Everyone will see how foolish he was.

"And they will laugh."

Ha ha ha

The Man Who Could Not Pay

That's too kind

Ome day, Jesus' friend Peter came to him. He had a question.
"If someone keeps treating me badly, how many times should I forgive? Is seven times too much?"

"It's not enough!" replied Jesus. "You must forgive seventy times seven."

Jesus told a story.

"There was once a king. He had lent money to his servants. Now he wanted to know how much they owed.

"There was one who owed him millions.

"'Please,' begged the servant. 'I can't pay.'

"'Can't pay?' said the king. 'Then I'll sell you as a slave. I'll sell your family if I need to.'

"'Please, no – be patient with me,' whimpered the servant.

"'Oh… all right. I'll let you off,' said the king.

There, there

Sob

"The servant went off. He knew he had been very lucky.

"Then he saw another servant. 'That man owes me money!' he exclaimed. He ran up to him and grabbed him.

"'Pay me what you owe. Pay me everything. Pay me now.'

"The second servant was dismayed.

"'Please give me more time,' he pleaded. 'I will pay.'

"The first servant did not show any pity. He had the second thrown into jail.

"The king heard what had happened. He ordered the first servant to come and see him.

"'I forgave you an enormous amount. You should have forgiven your friend. As you didn't – off to jail with you!'

"And that," said Jesus, "is what God will do if you do not forgive."

The Rich Fool

One day, a man spoke to Jesus from the crowd. "I know you are fair and honest. I need you to tell my brother that he's being unfair. I need you to tell him to share the money our father left us."

"That's not for me to say," replied Jesus.

Where shall I put the crops?

He turned to speak to everyone.

"Don't let yourself become greedy for money. It's not the things you have that matter."

He told a story.

"There was once a man who had a farm. Its fields produced good crops.

"'There isn't room in my barns for all this,' he said.

"Then he had an idea.

"'I'll pull down the old barns and build bigger ones.

"'Then I'll be wealthy for ever.

"'I'll be able to take life easy.'

Eat! Drink! Be merry!

"He was forgetting: life doesn't go on for ever. Just when he thought he was rich, he died. Someone else got all his money.

"That's what happens. So don't make money the most important thing in life. Make it your aim to live as a friend of God."

For me!
How nice!

The Friend at Midnight

Jesus often spent time saying prayers. His friends asked him to teach them to pray.

"Speak to God as to a loving father," he said.

"Tell God that you want him to be loved and obeyed by everyone.

"Ask God to give you the strength you need.

"Ask God to forgive the wrongs you have done.

"Ask God to keep you from hard times."

*Our Father
in heaven*

Then he told a story.

"Once a man was locking up his home for the night. As he stood behind the door, he heard a knock.

rat tat tat

"He opened the door, and there was a friend.

"'I was passing by on my journey,' cried the friend. 'I hope I can stay the night.'

"'Of course!' said the man. 'You are welcome.'

Nothing!

"He went to the kitchen. What food did he have to offer?

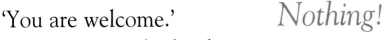

27

"He slipped out and ran next door. He knocked. He banged. He hammered.

"At last the neighbour stuck his head out of the window. 'Go away! We've all gone to bed,' he grumbled.

RAT TAT TAT

" 'But I need to borrow some food for a friend,' came the reply.

"The neighbour got up and stomped to the door with a basket of food.

"Remember," said Jesus. "Even a grumpy neighbour will do what you want if you ask enough.

"When you ask your Father God, you will be answered."

There

Ten Bridesmaids

"Do you want to be friends with God?" Jesus asked his listeners. "Then you must be ready always. No one knows when God will come to meet you.

"Once there were ten bridesmaids.

I brought extra lamp oil in case he's late

You won't need it

Their task was to welcome the bridegroom.

"He was expected at nightfall. The bridesmaids lit their lamps and waited.

"An hour went past. Two hours.

"The bridesmaids grew tired.

"They began to fall asleep.

"They were woken by a shout.

"'He's coming! Everyone get ready.'

"The bridesmaids jumped up. The five who had brought extra oil poured it into the lamps to make sure they went on burning brightly.

"The other five had almost no oil left.

"'Can we have some of yours?' they asked.

We must go and buy more

Can we borrow?

There's none spare

"The five girls who needed more oil hurried away. While they were gone, the bridegroom arrived.

"The five wise bridesmaids lifted their lamps high. They cheered as they followed the bridegroom into the feast.

"The five foolish bridesmaids came back too late. They were not even allowed in.

"So always be ready for God," said Jesus.

The Great Feast

Once Jesus was at a banquet. "This is good," said the man next to him. "But the feast that God gives his friends will be amazing!" Jesus told a story.

Today's the day!

"There was once a man who arranged a huge feast. He sent a messenger asking his friends if they would come. Then he got everything ready.

"On the day of the feast, the messenger went to remind the guests.

"One by one the guests began to make excuses.

Oh dear!

" 'I've just bought a plot of
land. I have to go and see it!'

Sorry

" 'I've bought some oxen.
I have to try them out.'

Sorry I forgot

" 'I just got married.
I really can't come.'

"When the man found out that the guests weren't coming, he was very upset.

" 'Everything is ready!' he cried. 'There's so much food!

" 'I know what I'll do,' he told his messenger. 'I want you to go into town and find all the poor people – beggars who can't walk, or can't see. Bring them to the feast.'

You're invited

What a treat!

Who, me?

"The guests arrived, but there was still room for more.

"'Please go out again,' the man asked his messenger.
'Go along the country roads and bring in the people you see.

"'As for the guests I first chose,' said the man, 'they won't
get a taste of this fantastic food.'"

The Runaway Son

I want it now

Some people complained about Jesus. "He doesn't choose his friends well. A lot of his followers are the wrong kind of people." Jesus told a story.

"There was once a man who had two sons. The younger was bored of working on the farm. He wanted to go and have fun in the city.

"'Please let me have my share of the family money,' he said.

"'It will be yours when I die,' said the father.

"The young man didn't want to wait.

Bye

Tra la la

"With a sigh, the father agreed. The young son sold the land that was now his. He went with his money to a city far away. There he enjoyed himself.

"Then the harvests failed. The price of food went up.
"The young man had been extravagant. Now his money had run out.

"He had to go and get a job. The only work he could get was looking after pigs.

"'I'm so miserable,' he wept. 'And hungry. I could eat the pig food.'

"Then he had an idea.

"'I shall go back to my father and say I'm sorry. I shall ask him to hire me as a servant.'

gobble

oink

Hurrah   He's alive

"He set off for home. He still had some way to go when his father saw him… and came running.

"'My son! You're back!' he cried.

"'I'm sorry for what I did,' mumbled the young man. 'Please take me on as a servant.'

"'But I love you!' cried the father. 'Servants… hurry! Get this boy new clothes… and make a feast.

"'We're going to have a party!'"

The Workers in the Vineyard

"One day," said Jesus, "God will welcome his friends into his kingdom. It will be like this."

A good wage

He told a story.

"There was a man who had a vineyard. The grapes were ripe, so he needed workers to harvest them.

"He went to the market in the early morning and hired some men.

"'I will pay a silver coin each for the day's work,' he said.

"They accepted.

"At nine o'clock, the man saw how much work was left.
"He went and hired more workers.

Agreed

One silver
coin each

"He did the same at noon, and again at three…
and then at five.

"When the day was over, everyone lined up to collect their pay.

"Those who had worked the shortest time each got a silver coin. Those who had worked the longest began to hope for more. But they too were paid one silver coin each.

"'We worked for hours!' they complained. 'It was hot during the day. We never stopped. That other lot only worked one hour.'

"'I am being fair,' said the man. 'I am paying what we agreed.'"

Jesus also told this story about God's kingdom.

"It is like a tiny seed," he said. "You can hardly see it.

"When it is sown, it grows into a huge tree. All kinds of birds come and make their home in its branches."

coo

chirrup

tweet

Rubber

Rubber

by Claire Llewellyn

W
FRANKLIN WATTS
A Division of Scholastic Inc.

First published in 2001 by
Franklin Watts
96 Leonard Street
London EC2A 4XD

First American edition 2002 by Franklin Watts
A Division of Scholastic Inc.
90 Sherman Turnpike
Danbury, CT 06816

ISBN 0-531-14628-6 (lib. bdg.) 0-531-14837-8 (pbk.)

Catalog details are available from the
Library of Congress Cataloging-in-Publication data

Series Editor: Rosalind Beckman
Series Designer: James Evans
Picture Research: Sue Mennell
Photography: Steve Shott

Printed in Hong Kong, China

Acknowledgments

Thanks are due to the following for kind permission to reproduce photographs:

Robert Harding Picture Library pp. 18b and back cover (John Miller), 16-17
Corbis Images pp. 8t (Chinch Gryniewicz/ Ecoscene), 15t (Charles E. Rotkin), 23t (Charles E. Rotkin), 27b (James Marshall)
Garden Matters p. 16 (Colin Milkins)
Harry Cory-Wright p. 15b
NASA p. 25
Popperfoto pp. 10 (Dave Joiner/PPP), 11b (Dave Joiner/PPP)
Still Pictures pp. 17 (Ron Giling), 18t (Mark Edwards), 19 (Ron Giling), 21t (Mark Edwards), 23b (Mark Edwards)
Telegraph Colour Library pp. 8b (Barry Willis), 12b (Chris Ladd), 14 (F.P.G./C.Benes), 26 (Curtis Martin), 27t (V.C.L.)
Tun Abdul Razak Research Centre pp. 20, 21b

Thanks are also due to the following for their help with this book: Barnard Associates Optometrists; International Rubber Study Group, London; John Lewis

Contents

Words printed in **bold italic** are explained in the glossary.

What Is Rubber?

Rubber is a very useful material. It is also a very safe material that can be used by everyone, even tiny babies.

Made of Rubber

Rubber is used to make thousands of different things. These things are all around us in houses, hospitals, factories, schools, swimming pools, offices, and cars.

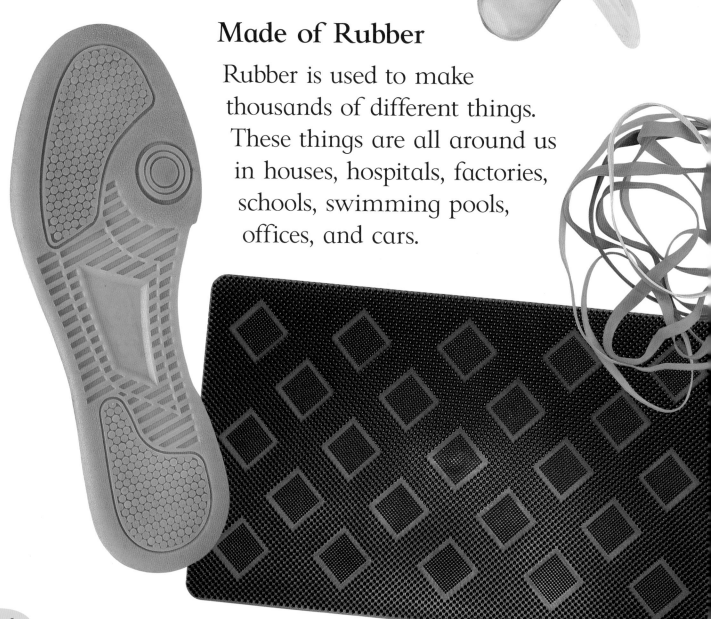

All the things in these pictures are made of rubber.
Can you name them all?

What do all these things feel like?
Do they all feel the same?

Fantastic Fact

The name rubber was given to the material because it can be used to rub out pencil.

Rubber Is Flexible and Stretchy

Rubber is different from most other materials because it can bend and stretch. This makes it very special.

A fireman's hose bends easily as it is aimed toward the fire.

The rubber hose on this paint sprayer allows it to reach every part of the car.

Things That Bend

Some materials are hard and stiff, but rubber is soft and flexible. This means it can easily bend and curl. Firemen's hoses are made of rubber so that they will bend easily to reach the fire. Some electric tools have cords made of rubber because it is strong and can be pulled around buildings.

Things That Stretch

When you pull rubber, it stretches. When you let it go, it springs back into shape. Swimming goggles have rubber straps. The strap stretches over your head, then springs back to give a good fit.

These goggles and swimming cap are made of rubber. They stretch to give a tight fit.

Try This

Blow up 3 balloons. Let the air out of the first one after 10 seconds; out of the second one after an hour; and out of the third one after 24 hours. Do all the balloons spring back into shape?

Rubber Is Springy

Rubber is a springy material.
It bounces off things that are hard.
It takes the shock out of bumps,
and helps keep things from breaking.

Bouncing About

If you drop a glass vase, it smashes on the ground. But if you drop a rubber ball, it will bounce back up again. Rubber's bounciness is a lot of fun. That's why rubber is used to make balls for tennis, basketball, and other games.

Many sports, such as tennis, are played with balls that have rubber inside them.

Keeping You Comfortable

Rubber is often used on the soles and heels of shoes. This makes shoes springy so they soak up the shock when your feet hit the ground. This makes walking more comfortable and helps protect the tiny bones in your feet.

Sneakers keep you comfortable and protect your feet.

Bicycle tires are tubes of rubber that are pumped full of air. The bouncy tires roll over bumps in the road for a more comfortable ride.

Bicycle tires are made to be comfortable even on long, hard journeys.

Fantastic Fact

The first bikes had wooden wheels that bumped along the road. They were so uncomfortable that they were called "bone-shakers."

Rubber Is Waterproof

Rubber is a **waterproof** material. It does not let water or other *liquids* through. It also stops bottles from leaking.

Keeping Dry

Rubber can be made into waterproof cloth. The cloth is perfect for babies' diapers and for mattress protectors in cribs. Rubber is also used to make all sorts of wet-weather gear, such as coats, trousers, and hats. A thin layer of rubber helps to waterproof other materials that often get wet, such as the cloth used for aprons and tablecloths.

Rubber gloves, trousers, and boots are helping to keep these people clean and dry.

Stopping Leaks

Rubber keeps water and air where you want them. Hot-water bottles are made of rubber to keep the water in. In the kitchen, rubber rings give a tight seal to bottles and jars.

Keeping Water Out

Water and *electricity* must be kept apart. A waterproof rubber cord keeps water locked out and dangerous electricity locked in.

Try This

Test whether rubber is waterproof. Fill a rubber glove with water. Does any of the water drip through?

Rubber Is Strong

Rubber is a very strong, durable material. It is sometimes used in machines and buildings that get a lot of use.

Preventing Damage

Rubber is often used as a building material in bridges and **skyscrapers**. It helps make them more stable. In places where there are **earthquakes**, rubber is often used in the **foundations** of buildings. It helps to absorb, or soak up, the shock of the earthquake and lessen the damage.

Los Angeles, California, is in an area where there are many earthquakes. Rubber is used in the foundations of the buildings to prevent them from collapsing.

Tough and Strong

Rubber is used on *conveyor belts* and moving pavements because it is flexible and very strong.

A conveyor belt easily moves these coils of rubber tubing from one part of the factory to another.

Rubber also makes a durable floor covering. It is often used in busy public places such as stations and airports. It is springy to walk on, gives a good grip for shoes, and helps cut down on noise.

Fantastic Fact

The largest trucks have rubber tires that are nearly 12 feet (4 meters) high. Even a tall person reaches only halfway up a tire.

Rubber tires have to be tough because they carry a lot of weight.

15

Rubber Comes from Trees

Rubber is a **natural** material. It is made from **latex**, a milky white juice that is found inside plants.

The Rubber Tree

Latex is found in many plants. The latex in the rubber tree contains more rubber than any other plant. The scientific name of the rubber tree is *hevea*, but most people just call it the rubber tree.

Some plants run with latex if you cut them, as this picture shows.

Rubber *Plantations*

Rubber trees are narrow, straight, and tall. They grow in places near the **equator**, in the warmest, wettest parts of the world. Most of the world's rubber comes from trees that are grown in huge plantations in the **Far East**.

The fully grown trees of a rubber plantation

Fantastic Fact

Wild rubber trees were first found in South America. People took seeds from these trees and then planted them in other parts of the world. This is how plantations started.

This is a new rubber plantation. In time these plants will grow as tall as the trees in the picture at the top of the page.

Collecting the Latex

Latex is easy to collect. Plantation workers make a cut in the bark of a rubber tree and wait for the latex to drip out. This is known as "tapping" the tree.

Plantation workers use a special curved knife to cut into the rubber tree.

Tapping the Tree

The latex inside a rubber tree flows in tiny tubes inside the bark. To collect the latex, plantation workers make a thin, curving cut in the bark, then fix a *spout* and a cup at the bottom. Latex drips along the cut and into the cup. Rubber trees can be tapped when they are seven years old. They will produce latex for about thirty years.

The milky latex runs into the cup.

Collecting the Latex

When the cups are full, they are emptied into buckets. Latex spoils easily after tapping, so it must be made into solid rubber as soon as possible. This is usually done at the plantation.

Collecting the latex. A rubber tree is tapped every four days.

Fantastic Fact

A rubber tree produces up to 4 gallons (15 liters) of latex a year.

From Latex to Rubber

Solid rubber is separated from the latex. It is made into sheets or blocks, packed up, and shipped all over the world.

The lumps of rubber form at the back of the tank.

Removing the Rubber

The latex is poured into long, narrow tanks, where it is strained to remove bits of dirt. *Acid* is then added to the tanks. The acid turns the rubber in the latex into solid lumps, which rise up and float on the surface.

Try This

Put 2 tablespoons of milk into a glass and stir in 2 tablespoons of vinegar. After a few seconds, you will see that the acid in the vinegar makes the milk turn lumpy. This is what happens when acid is added to latex.

Making Rubber Sheets

The rubber lumps are passed through rollers. The rollers squeeze out the water and press the lumps into rubbery sheets. At the factory, the sheets are hung up in warm rooms to dry for several days. Then they are made into **bales**, loaded onto ships, and sent to factories around the world.

Rubber is often processed next to the plantation. Rollers are used to squeeze the rubber into flat sheets, which are hung up and left to dry.

Blocks of rubber are pressed together to make bales.

21

Making Rubber Things

The bales of dry rubber arrive at the factory. Here the rubber is treated and shaped to make many different things.

Treating the Rubber

Dry rubber is treated in different ways. It is mixed with other materials and heated to make it soft and easy to handle. It is also mixed with chemicals. Different chemicals can make rubber hard or strong, or as springy as a sponge.

The rubber of a bottle is strong enough for a baby to suck and chew on.

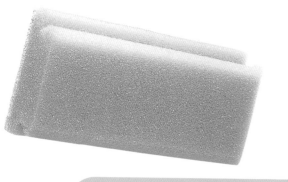

The sponge and the foam rubber inside the cushion feel soft because they contain thousands of tiny air bubbles. You can see these air bubbles in the close-up picture of the foam rubber.

Shaping the Rubber

Rubber can be made into many different shapes. It is rolled flat for flooring or doormats. It is squeezed through holes to make pipes and tubes. It is pushed into **molds** to make things such as hot-water bottles and tires.

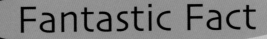

These tires have been shaped in a mold.

Fantastic Fact

Thin, stretchy things such as balloons are made from latex instead of dry rubber. Molds are dipped into the liquid latex before being left to dry.

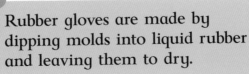

Rubber gloves are made by dipping molds into liquid rubber and leaving them to dry.

Rubber Without Trees

Not all rubber is made from latex.
It can also be made from chemicals.
This material is known as
synthetic rubber.

kitchen spatula

Using Chemicals

About one hundred years ago, scientists
began to study natural rubber.
They examined its chemical makeup
to see how it was made. Over
the years they have learned to
copy it by using chemicals made
from oil. These chemicals
make a material that is like
natural rubber, and can often
be used in its place. Many items
that people use every day are
made of synthetic rubber.

teething ring

potato peeler

Synthetic Rubber

Scientists are always searching for new materials. They have **experimented** with various chemicals to make new kinds of synthetic rubber. Some of these materials are stronger than natural rubber and can handle hotter temperatures. This means synthetic rubber can be used in spaceships, power stations, and other places where natural rubber cannot.

Natural rubber is not strong enough to stand the heat and cold of space. A special type of synthetic rubber is used instead.

Fantastic Fact

More than half of all the rubber we now use is synthetic. It is cheaper to make than natural rubber.

Recycling Rubber

Most of the world's rubber is used to make tires. Millions of them are made every year. Getting rid of old tires is a serious problem. **Recycling** could be the answer.

Getting Rid of Tires

It is not easy to get rid of old tires because rubber does not rot. Burying or burning old tires makes *gases* that *pollute* the air. Storing tires is a fire risk, and it provides shelter for rats and other pests.

Part of a huge dump of unwanted tires

Recycling Tires

Old tires can be cut up into tiny chips. These can be used to make floor coverings or a safe rubber surface for playgrounds or running tracks. They can also be used in pavements, runways, and roads. Rubber makes these surfaces quieter and helps them last longer.

An old tire makes the perfect swing.

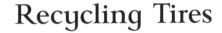

This path of recycled rubber makes it easy to walk on the sand.

Fantastic Fact

There are about 2 billion old tires in the United States alone, and 250 million more are added every year.

Glossary

acid   a strong substance with a sharp or sour taste. Some acids are poisonous. Vinegar is a mild acid and is safe to use with food.

bale   a large bundle

conveyor belt   a moving rubber belt used in places such as factories and airports to move things along

earthquake   a sudden movement deep inside the Earth. Earthquakes make the ground shake, damaging buildings and bridges.

electricity   a useful kind of energy that can be used to make heat and light and power a motor

equator   an imaginary line around the middle of the Earth, halfway between the North and South Poles

experiment   to try out something new

Far East   a part of the world that contains many countries, including Thailand, Malaysia, Indonesia, and China

flexible   able to bend easily

foundation	the solid stonework under a building. Foundations are built in holes in the ground to support the building above.
gas	a substance that is neither a liquid nor a solid, such as air
latex	the thick, milky juice in rubber plants
liquid	a runny substance, such as water, that takes on the shape of the container it is in
mold	a container with a special shape
natural	found in the world around us
plantation	a large piece of land that is used to grow one type of plant, such as rubber trees
pollute	to spoil or poison the air, land, or water with harmful substances
recycle	to take a used object or material and make something else
skyscraper	a tall building with many floors
spout	a small tube that is fixed to a rubber tree to help the latex flow into a cup
synthetic	not natural; made by people
waterproof	not letting water through

Index